WHAT KEEPS YOUR BRILLIANT BODY WORKING?

Written by John Farndon
Illustrated by Alan Rowe

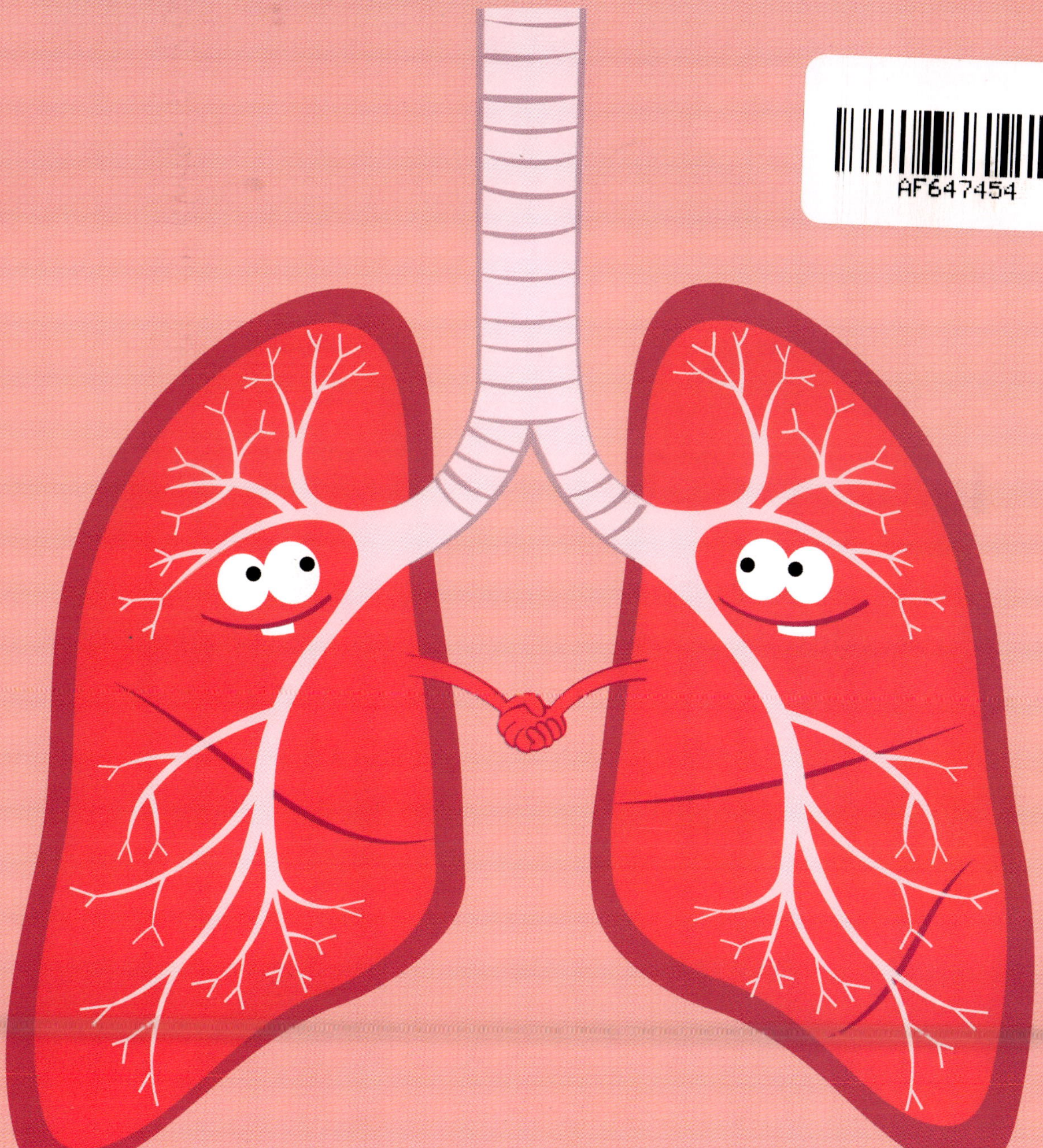

First published in 2023 by Hungry Tomato Ltd
F15, Old Bakery Studios, Blewetts Wharf, Malpas Road, Truro, Cornwall, TR1 1QH, UK.

A CIP catalogue record for this book is available from the British Library.

Published and Distributed in India by Scholastic India Pvt. Ltd.

ISBN 978-93-5954-126-6

This reprint edition : January 2025

Printed in India at Shree Maitrey Printech Pvt. Ltd., Noida

Discover more at
www.hungrytomato.com

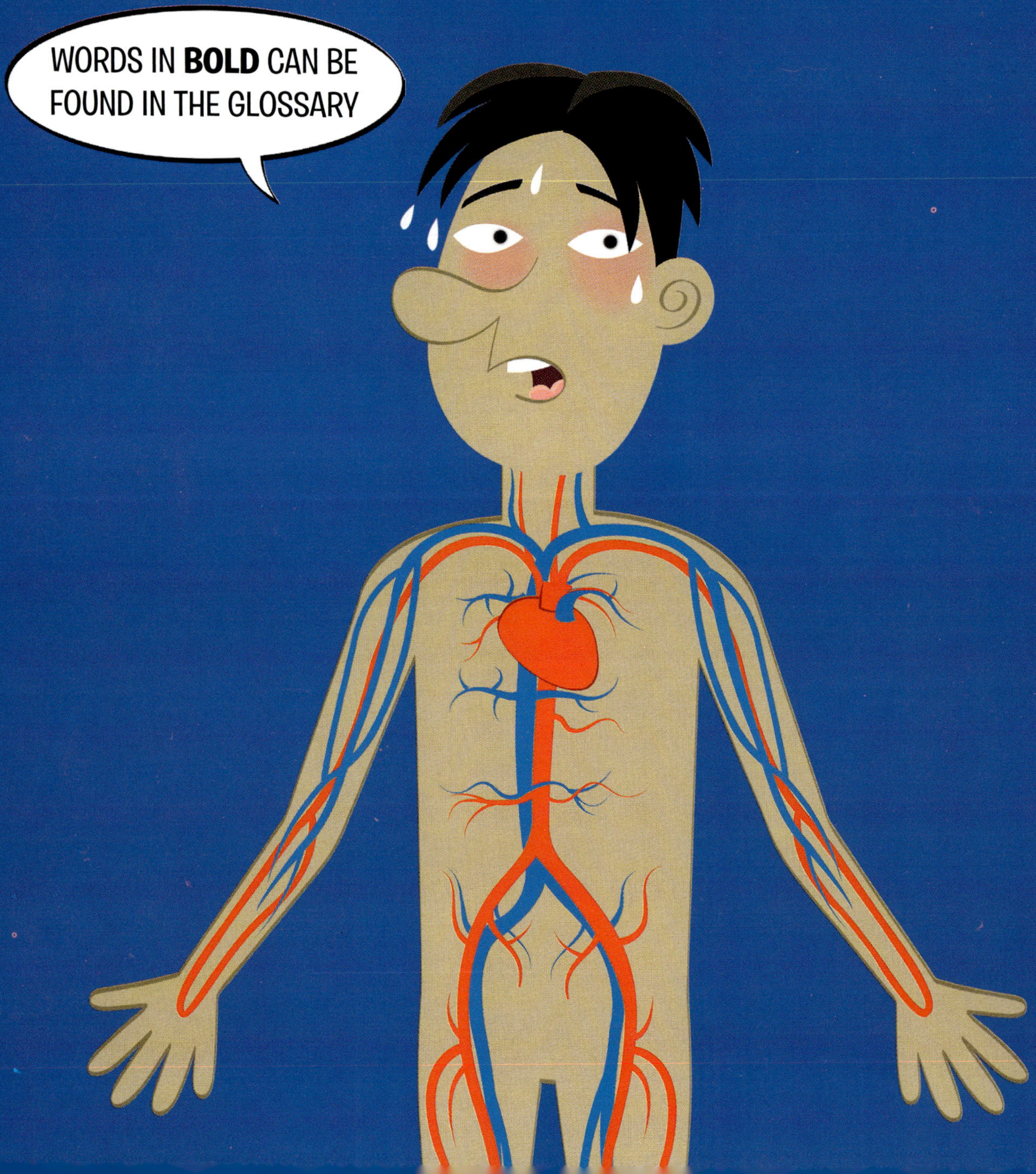

CONTENTS

WHAT ARE YOU MADE OF?	4
TAKE A DEEP BREATH	6
KEEP THE BEAT	8
BLOOD CAROUSEL	10
LIFE JUICE	12
GETTING SICK	14
GERM BATTLES	16
GOT A CURE?	18
SNOT AND SNEEZES	20
GLOSSARY	22
INDEX	23

WHAT ARE YOU MADE OF?

All bodies are made of simple materials. It's how they're put together that makes you so special!

What's your body made of?

Mostly water! But it's all held in place by a crowd of tiny, smart, squishy packages called cells. There are more than 37 trillion of them! Here are some different kinds:

Red blood cell

Muscle cell

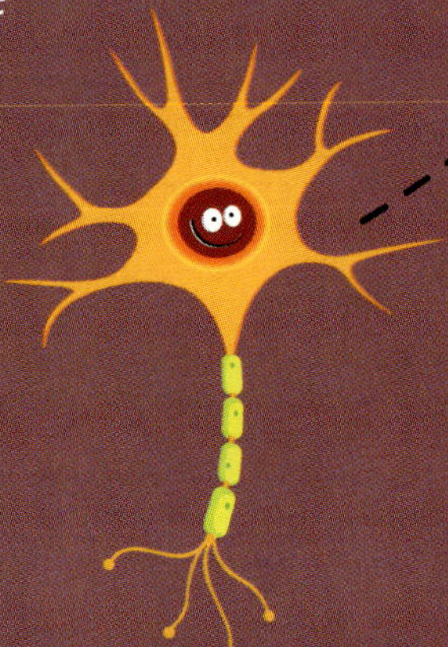

Nerve cell (neuron)

Fat cell

Liver cell

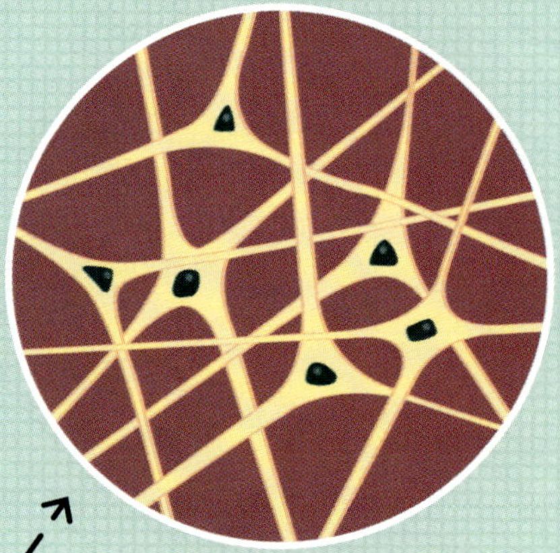

Nervous tissue

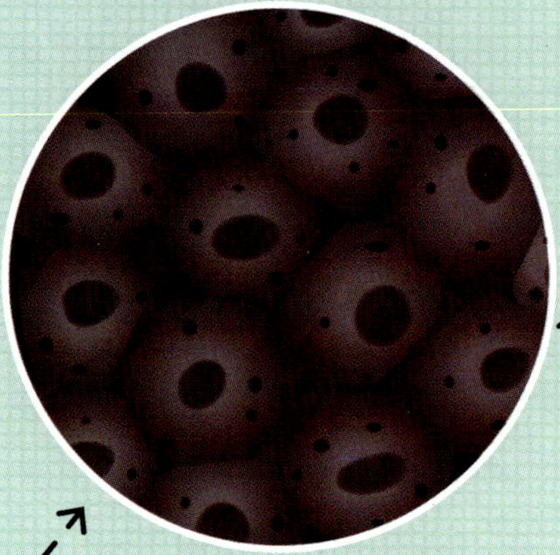

Liver tissue

How does it all fit together?

Similar cells grow together to make tissues, such as **muscles**, bones and skin. Connective tissue connects different parts of the body together. The spaces between are usually filled with liquid.

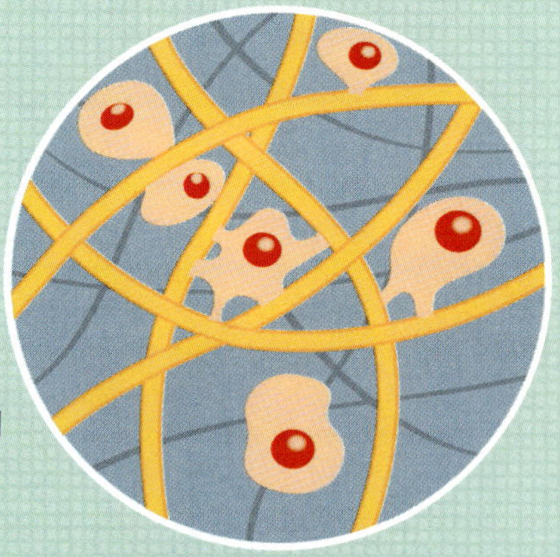

Connective tissue

What are organs?

Organs are special parts of your body with their own tasks, such as your eyes, heart, lungs, liver and stomach.

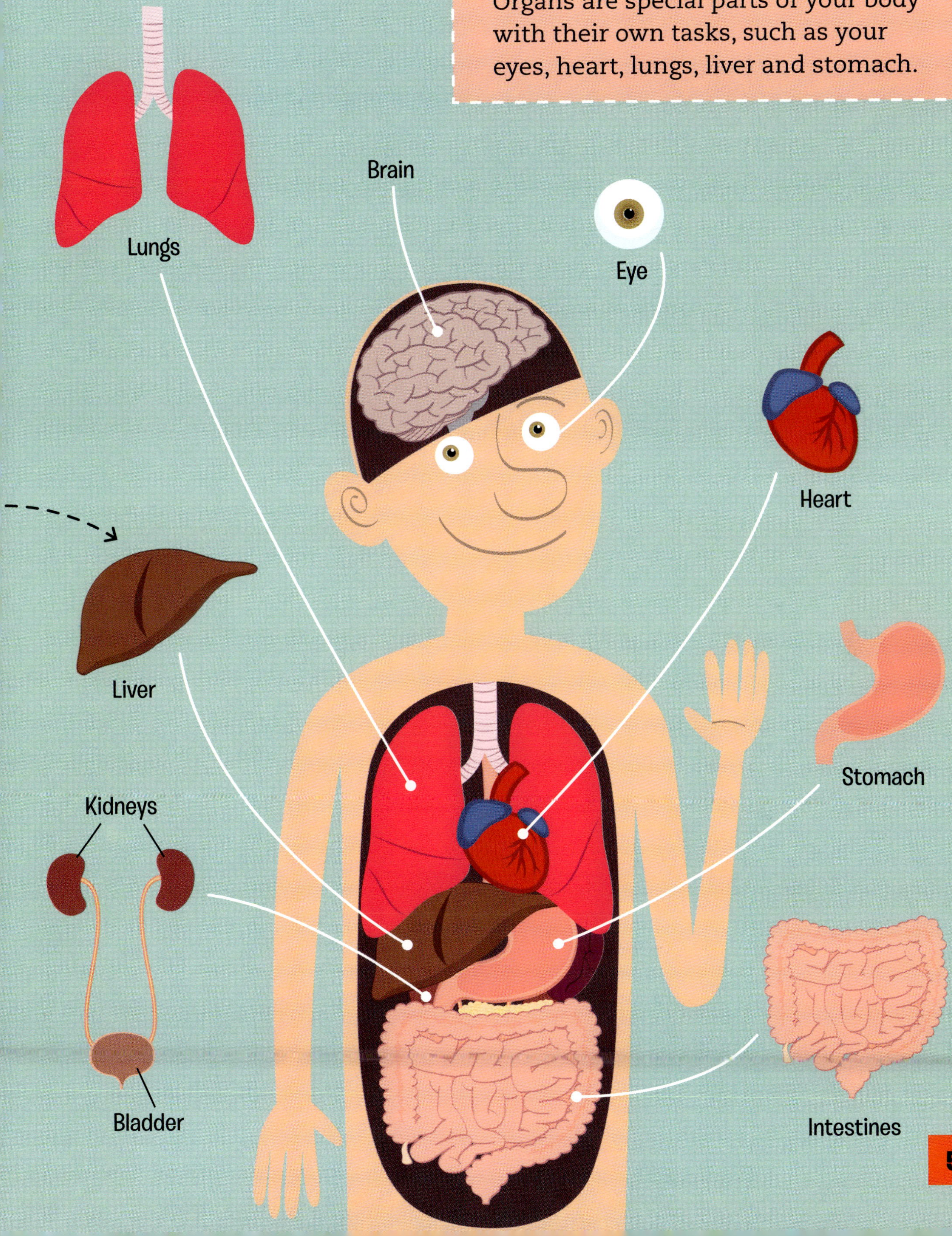

TAKE A DEEP BREATH

You want to know the secret of staying alive? Don't hold your breath for too long!

Why do you need to breathe?

Your body needs **oxygen**, a gas found in the air. It helps power every part of you. Without a constant supply, things quickly stop working.

What are lungs?

You have two lungs. They are big rubbery sacks containing thousands of tiny tubes, called **airways**, which branch out like a tree. Their important job (as well as breathing) is to send oxygen into your blood.

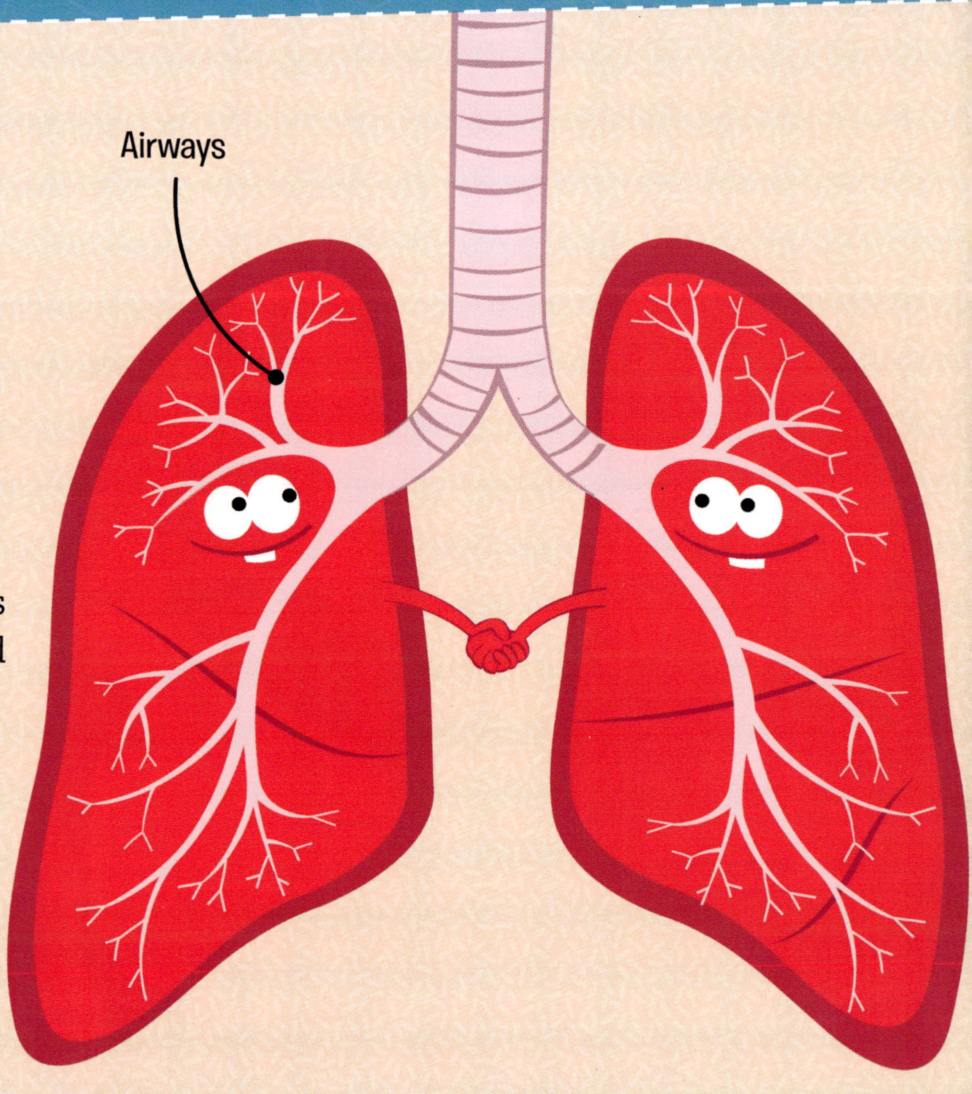

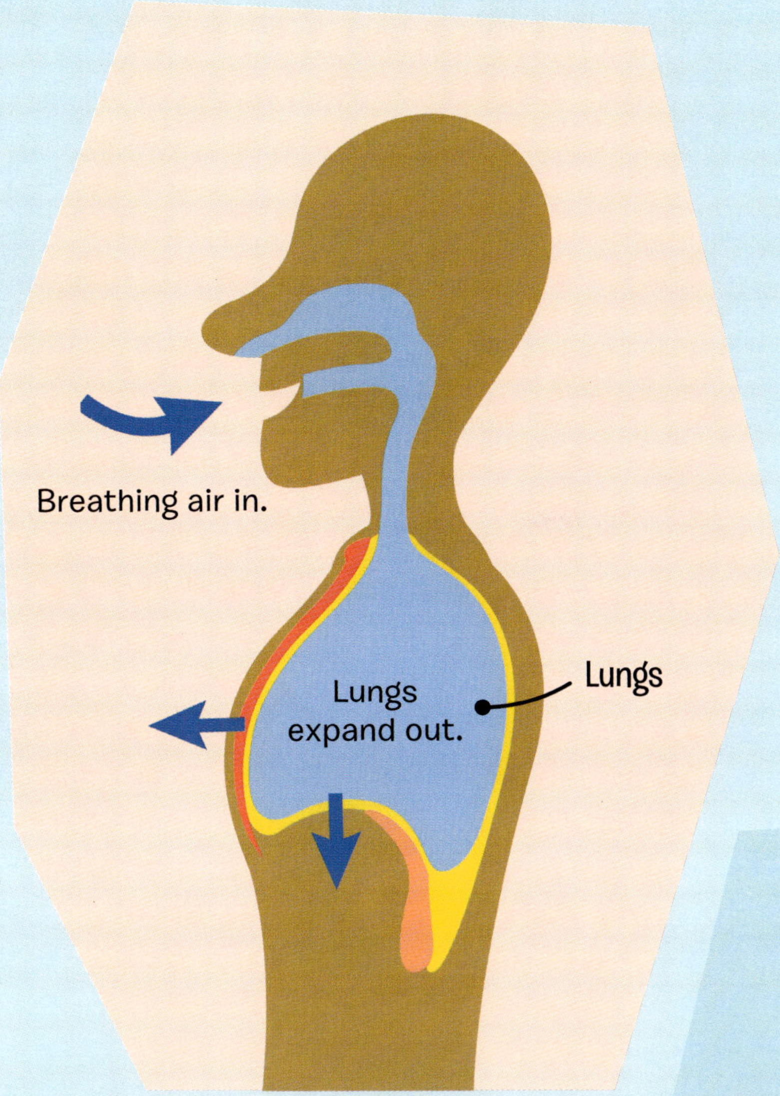

What happens when you breathe in?

When you breathe in, your lungs inflate like a balloon, sucking air in through your nose and mouth, and down into your lungs, which quickly take oxygen from it.

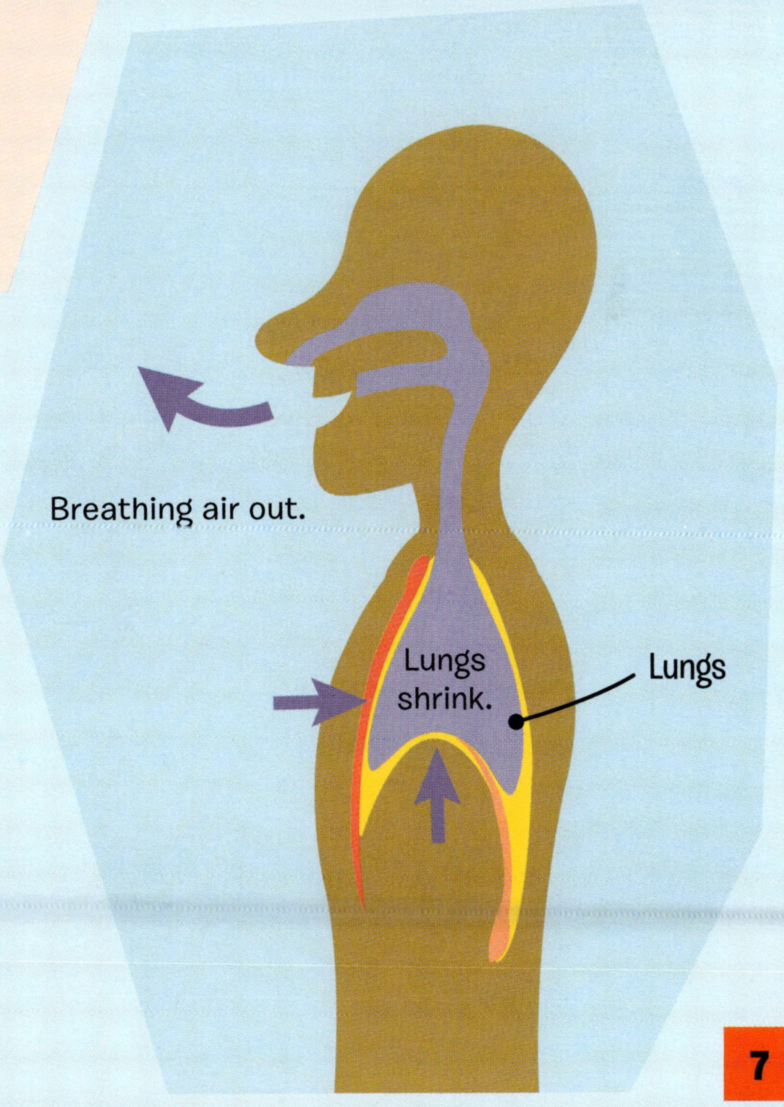

What happens when you breathe out?

To breathe out, your lungs let the air go again, along with unwanted carbon dioxide, a gas made by your body.

KEEP THE BEAT

Press your fingers on the middle of your chest. Can you feel your heart beating?

What is your heart?

Your heart is a little pump in the middle of your chest. It's made of muscle that tightens and relaxes all the time to pump blood around your body.

How does your heart work?

When your heart muscle relaxes, blood rushes in. When the muscle tightens it pushes blood out.

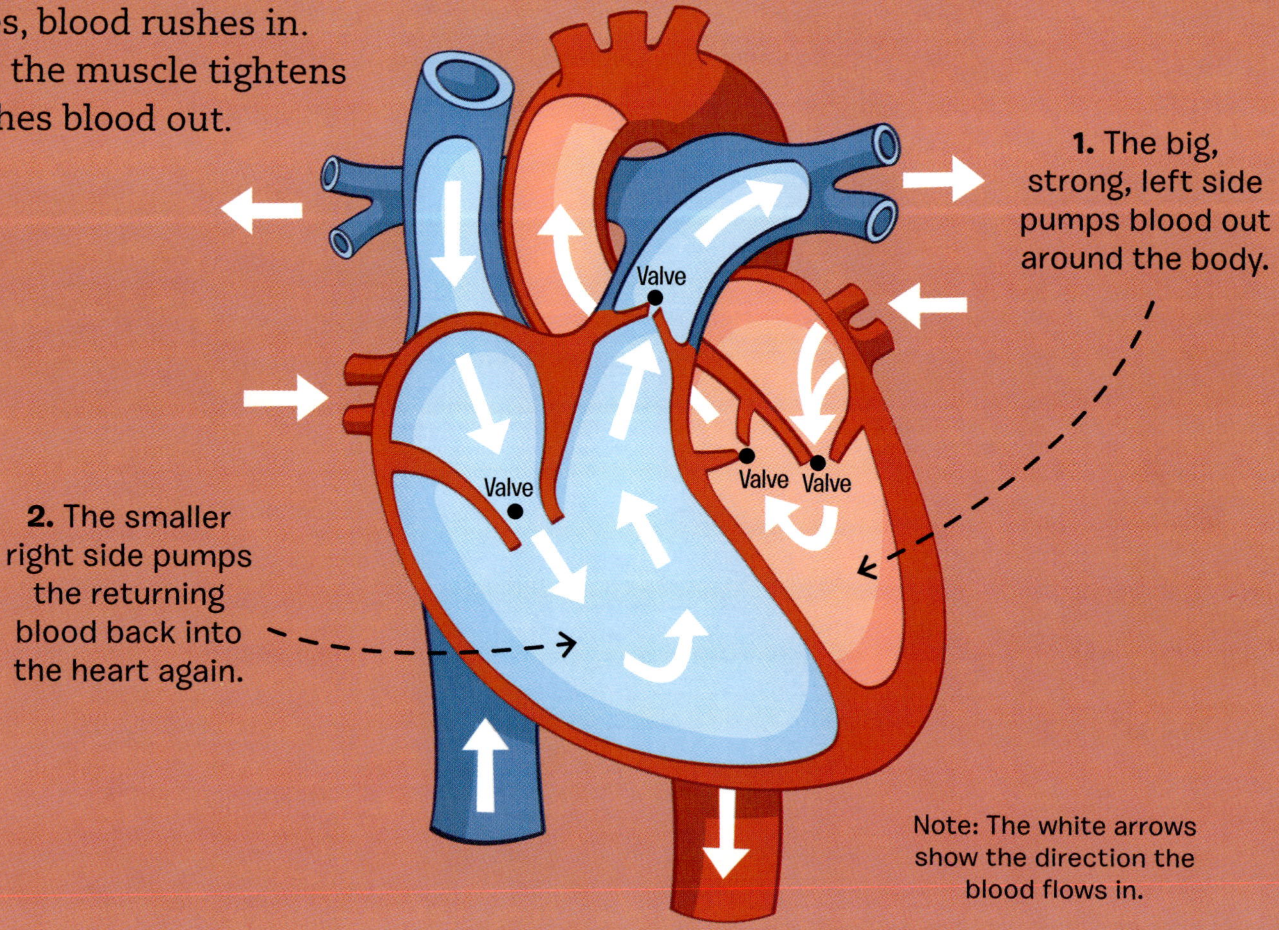

Note: The white arrows show the direction the blood flows in.

Why can you hear your heartbeat?

Every time blood is pushed out, little flaps inside your heart, called valves, slam shut like doors to stop it from flowing back the wrong way. The thumping noise of your heartbeat is the sound of the valves slamming shut.

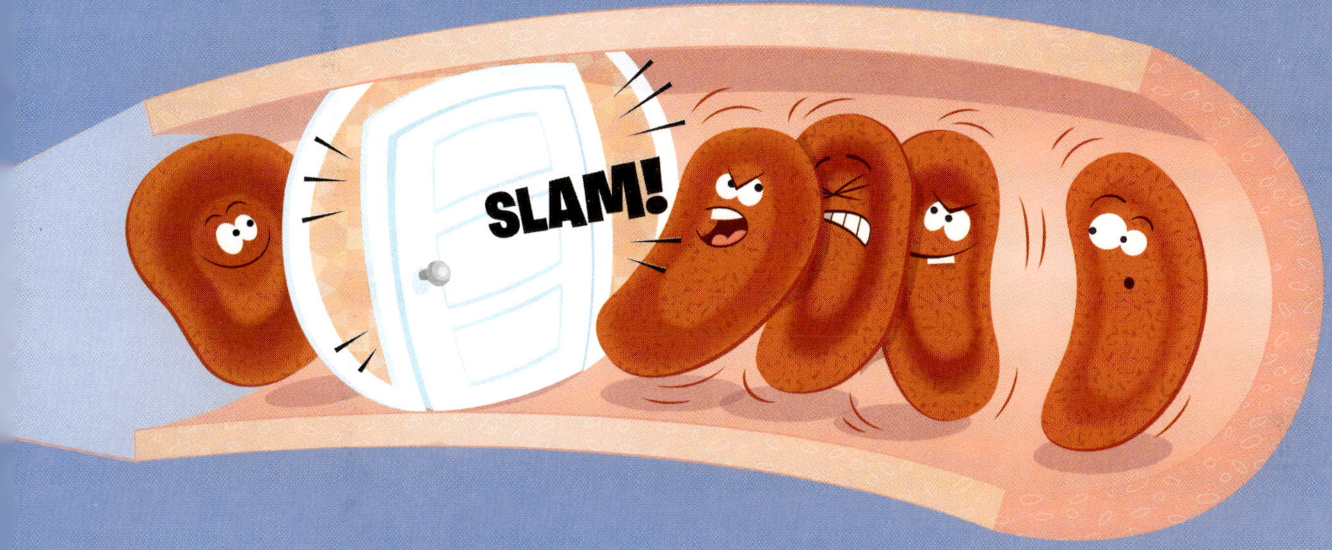

How fast does your heart beat?

Your heart normally beats about 75 times a minute. But when you run, it starts pumping faster to supply your muscles with the extra oxygen they need.

You can feel each little push, or pulse, of your blood, by touching the inside of your wrist. You could even try counting how many beats you feel in a minute.

BLOOD CAROUSEL

Your body is full of red liquid called blood, but what's it for?

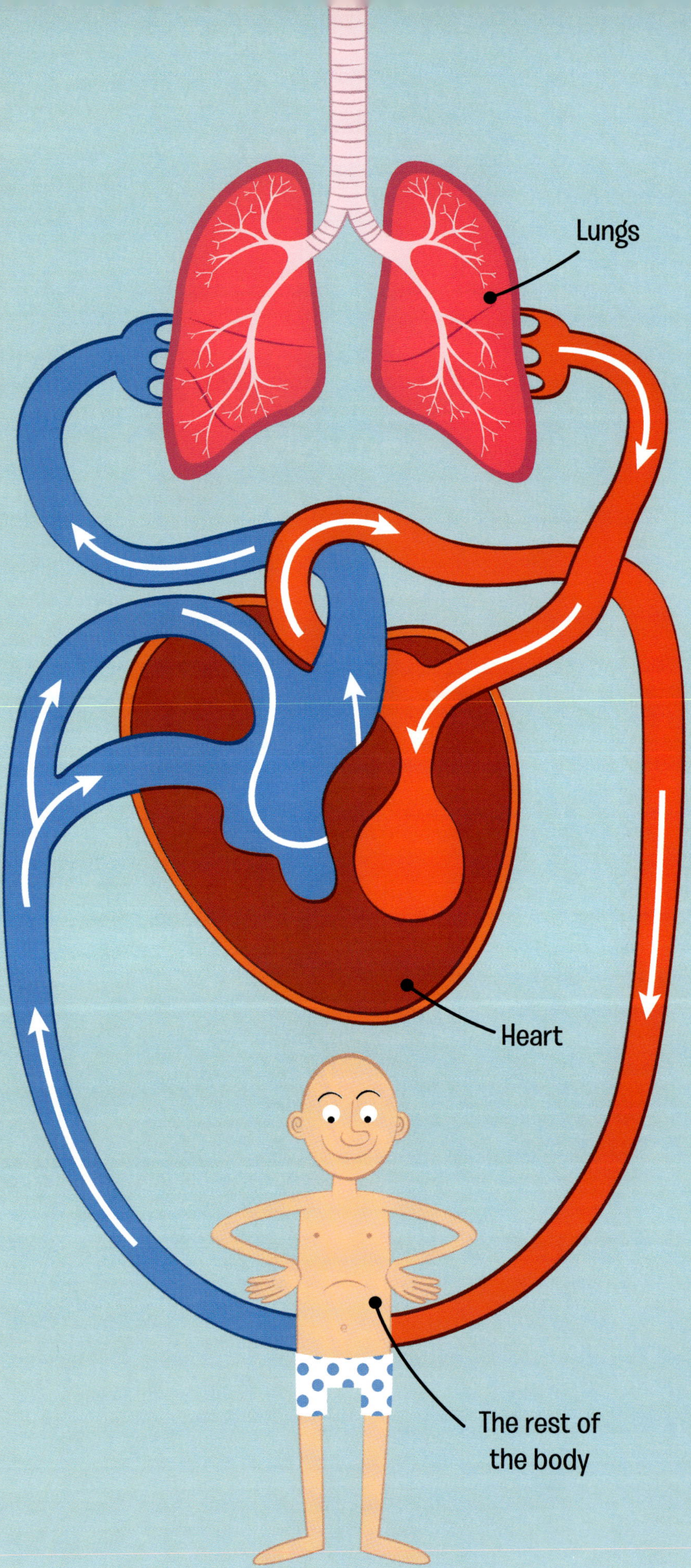

What does blood do?

Its main job is to carry oxygen from your lungs to every part of your body. Your heart pumps it around through pipes called blood vessels. This is called circulation.

- **Out**: Blood carries oxygen from the lungs to the body.
- **Back**: Blood carries unwanted carbon dioxide waste back to the lungs.

What are arteries and veins?

These are the biggest blood vessels. Arteries carry blood loaded with oxygen away from the lungs. Veins carry blood back. The oxygen makes the blood in arteries bright red.

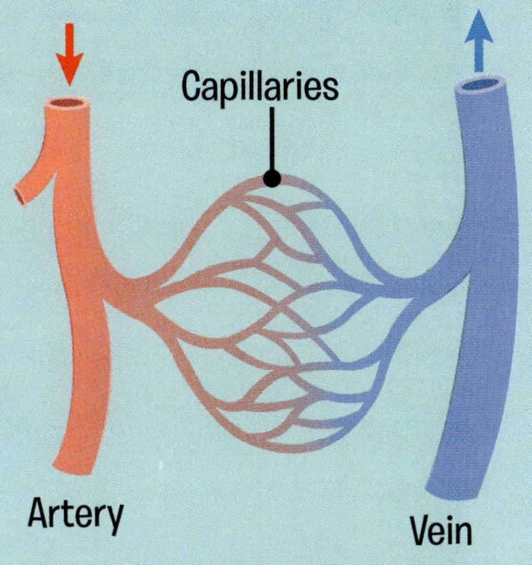

Why do some people go red when they're hot?

Your tiniest blood vessels are called capillaries. When you're hot, more blood runs into the capillaries in your skin to cool off, making your skin look redder.

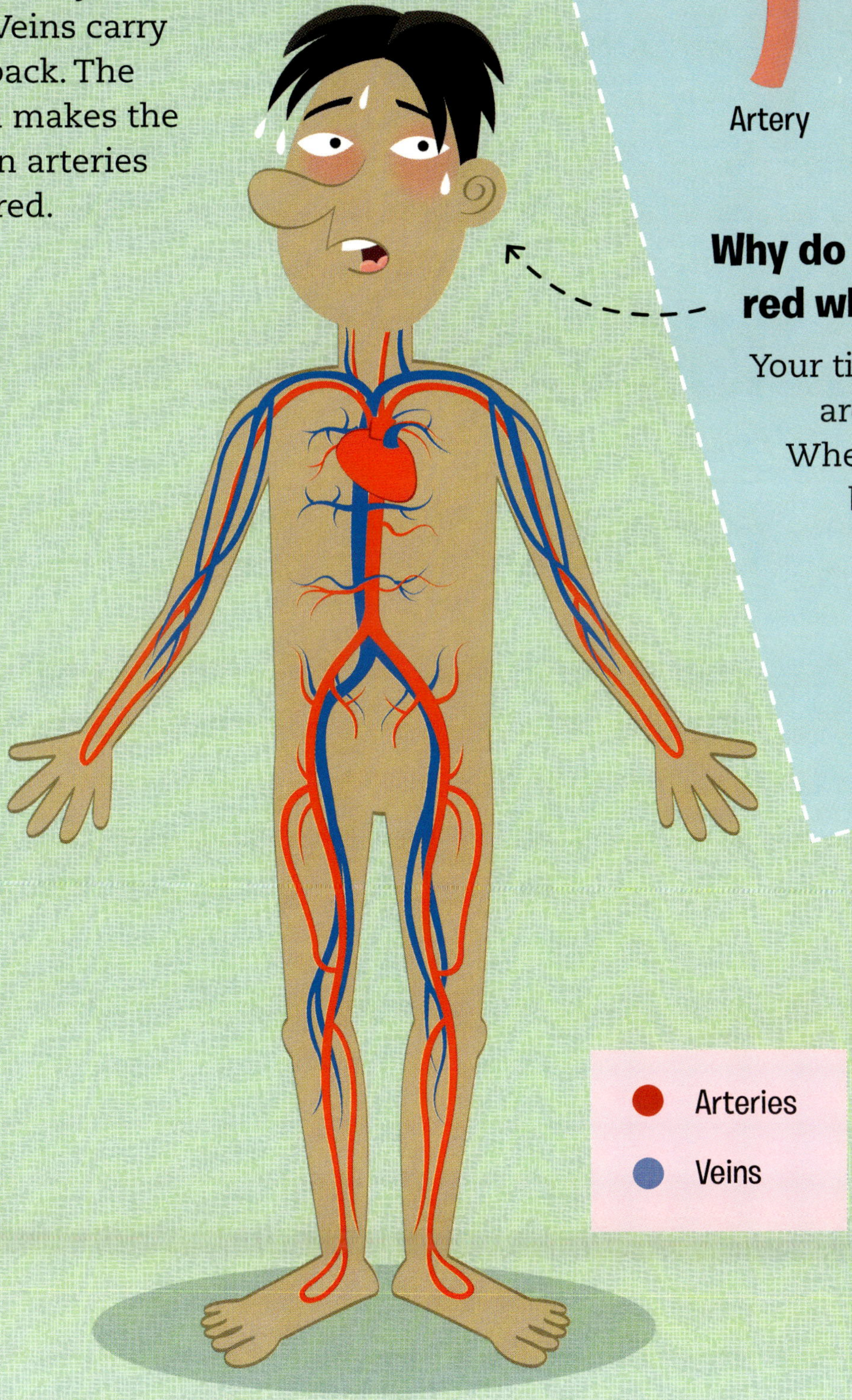

LIFE JUICE

Blood looks just like red ink, doesn't it? But what's it really made of?

What's in blood?

Your blood is like a soup full of useful substances that need to be carried around the body.

White blood cells

They help your body fight **germs**.

Plasma

It is the watery part of your blood.

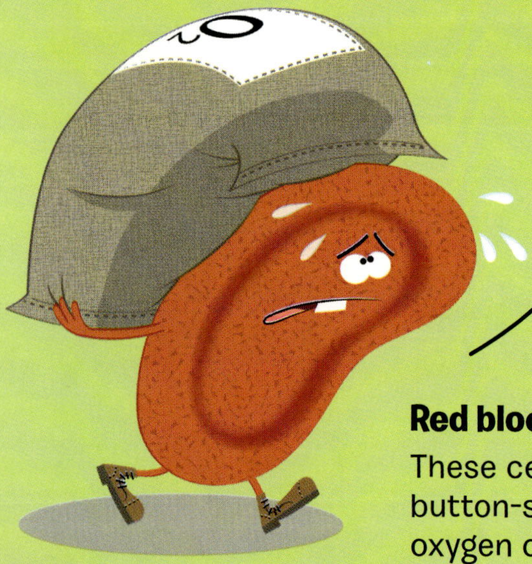

Platelets

They are the emergency team for fixing any damage.

Red blood cells

These cells are button-shaped oxygen carriers.

How much blood do you have?

The average adult has enough blood in their body to fill about 15 to 16 cans of cola.

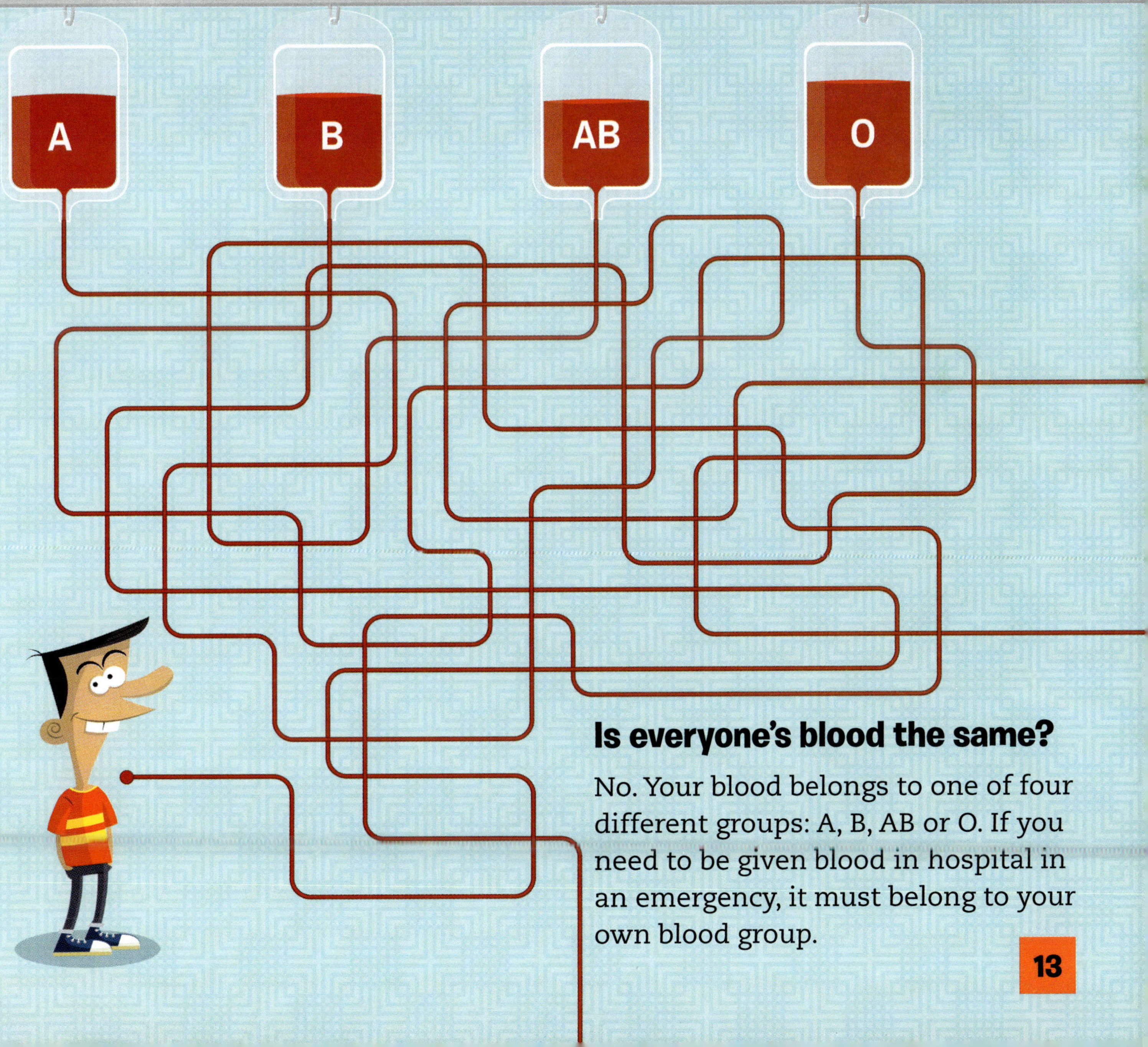

Is everyone's blood the same?

No. Your blood belongs to one of four different groups: A, B, AB or O. If you need to be given blood in hospital in an emergency, it must belong to your own blood group.

GETTING SICK

Being sick is never fun. What actually makes you ill?

What are germs?

Germs are **microbes** that are so small they're basically invisible! They may be tiny, but when they get into your body, they can multiply and make you sick. The main germs are bacteria and viruses.

What are bacteria?

Bacteria are tiny living things made from just one cell. Millions are harmless, but there are a few that are really bad news! Here are some mean ones and some of the diseases they cause:

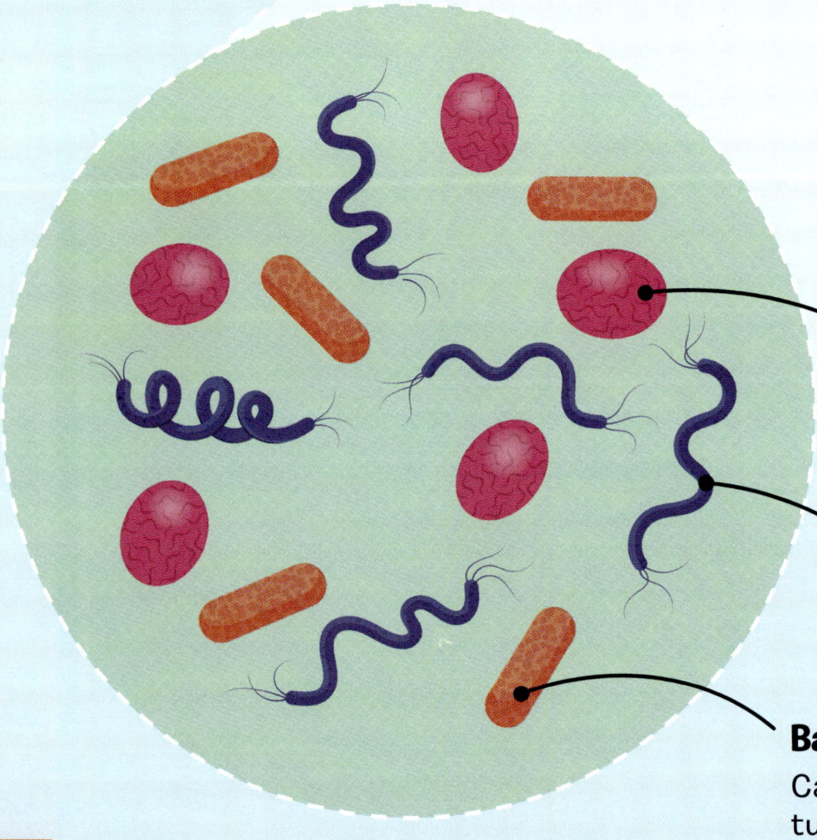

Cocci

Causes pneumonia, scarlet fever and meningitis.

Spirilla

Causes upset stomachs.

Bacilli

Causes tetanus, tuberculosis (TB), whooping cough and diphtheria.

What are viruses?

Viruses are so tiny you need high-powered microscopes to see them. They can't live by themselves, but invade cells in your body and take them over.

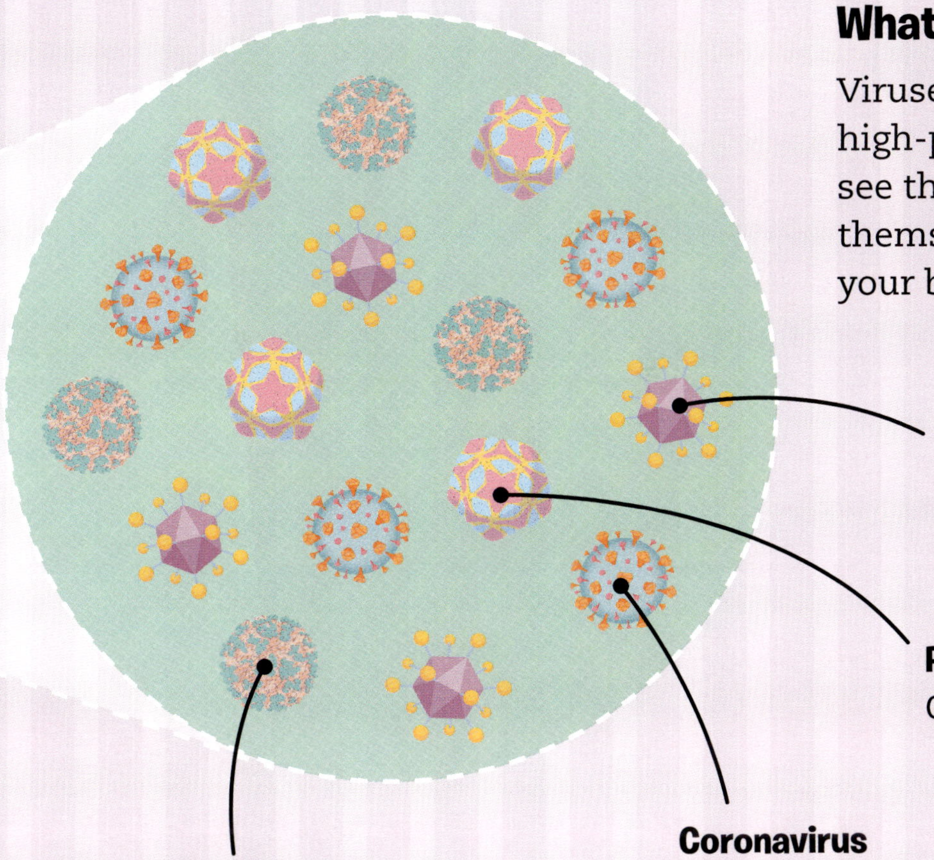

Why do germs make me feel bad?

They can damage your body by releasing poisons or upsetting how your body works. But fever (hotness) and aches are signs that your body is fighting off the germs.

GERM BATTLES

When you get infected by germs, it can be nasty. So how does your body fight back?

How do germs get in?

Your skin keeps most germs out, but they can get into your body through cuts, and through your eyes, nose and mouth.

What happens if germs get in?

You have an army of white blood cells to fight germs.

They can identify germs at once by their antigens, which act like ID tags, and go on the attack.

Some big white blood cells swallow germs whole!

GOT A CURE?

Viruses can cause your body lots of problems, but luckily you have secret weapons to fight them, called antibodies.

What are antibodies?

Sneaky viruses hide away inside cells in your body, but they leave antigens on their surface.

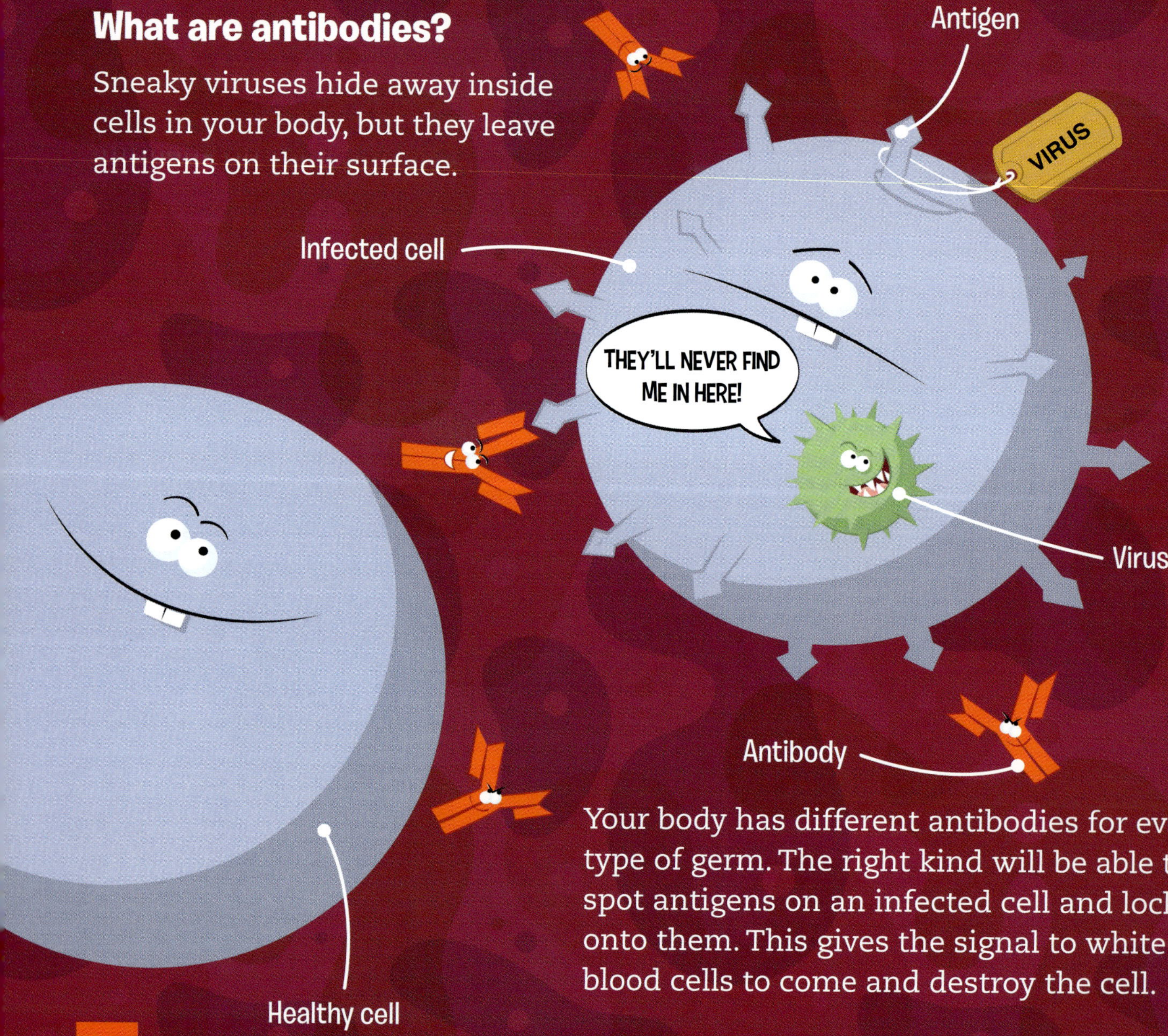

Your body has different antibodies for every type of germ. The right kind will be able to spot antigens on an infected cell and lock onto them. This gives the signal to white blood cells to come and destroy the cell.

When germs are found, the right antibodies multiply like mad and hunt them down.

What is a vaccine?

Vaccines help stop you getting ill by giving you a harmless version of a germ. Your body reacts by building a store of antibodies, ready to fight off the real germ.

SNOT AND SNEEZES

Let's get nosy and find out what's going on up your nose!

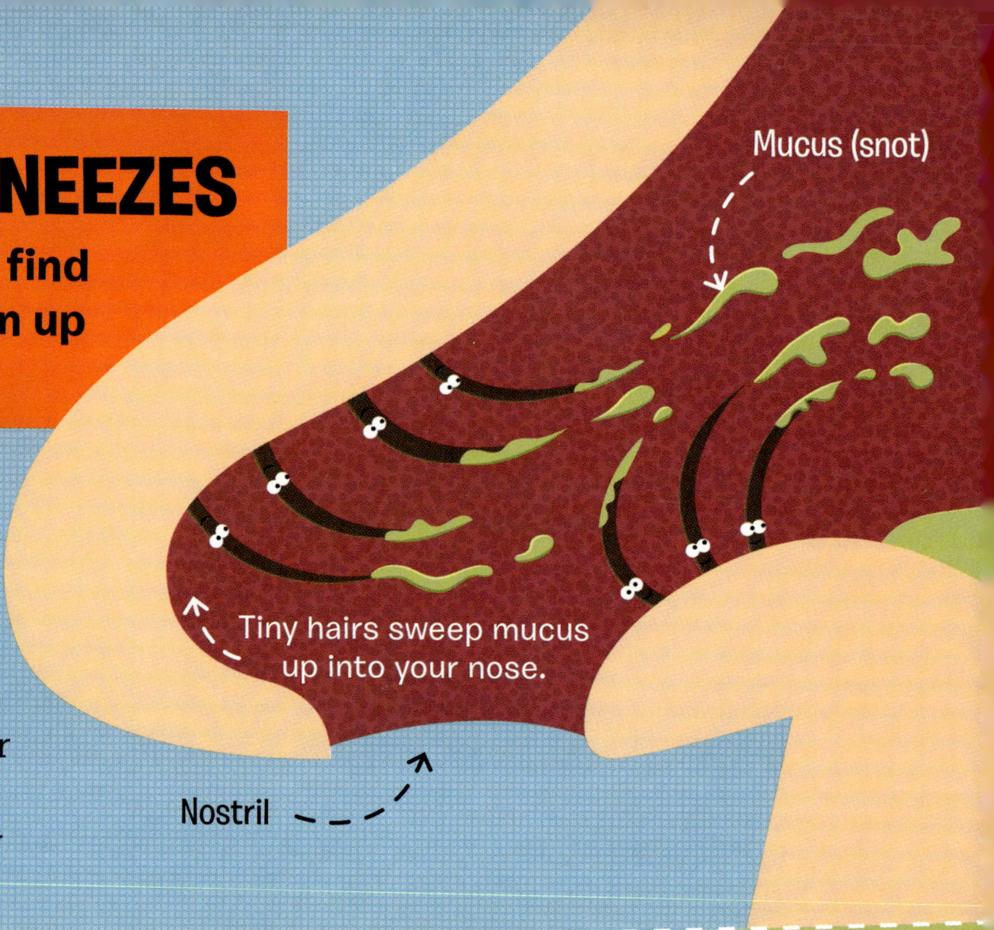

What is snot?

Snot is mostly water, with oils to make it thick and slimy, and some stuff that helps fight infection. Its proper name is mucus and it protects your airways by trapping germs and dirt.

Why does my nose run?

If you have a cold, your nose goes into snot overdrive to keep out germs. It can react the same way to things you are allergic to, such as pollen, thinking they are germs.

Cold weather can make your nose run, too!

Snot gets filled with junk that you breathe in, such as dust, pollen, germs, sand, smoke and particles from outer space!

Why do we sneeze?

It's your nose and airway's way of rebooting, like when you restart a computer. Sneezing clears out all the mucky mess so that you can start fresh.

How many times can you sneeze?

The world record for sneezing is held by a girl named Donna Griffiths, who sneezed one million times in a row, for two and a half years, between 1981 and 1983!

GLOSSARY

airways
The tubes that run from your nose and mouth to your lungs, which you breathe through. The tiny tubes inside your lungs are also called airways.

germs
Tiny living things, including bacteria and viruses, that can make you ill if they get inside your body.

infected
When your body has been invaded by germs that can cause it harm.

microbes
Tiny living things, such as germs, which are too small to see without using a microscope.

muscles
Muscles are bundles of rope-like tissue that tighten and relax to make your body move. You have more that 650 muscles all over your body.

oxygen
A gas found in the air that most living things need to live.

INDEX

A
airways 6, 20-21, 22
antibodies 18-19
antigens 17, 18
arteries 11

B
bacteria 14
bladder 5
blood 4, 6, 8-13, 17, 18
blood vessels 10-11
bones 4
brain 5
breathing 6-7, 21

C
capillaries 11
cells 4, 12, 14-15, 17-19

E
eye 15, 16

F
fat cell 4

G
germs 12, 14-21, 22

H
heart 5, 8-10

I
infections 16-18, 20, 22
intestines 5

K
kidneys 5

L
liver 5
lungs 5, 6-7, 10-11

M
microbes 14-22
mouth 7. 16
muscles 4, 8-9, 22

N
nerve cell (neuron) 4
nose 7, 16, 20-21

O
organs 5
oxygen 6-7, 9-12, 22

P
plasma 12
platelets 12

R
red blood cell 4, 12

S
skin 4, 11, 16
sneeze 20-21
snot 20-21
stomach 5

T
tissues 4

V
vaccine 19
veins 11
virus 14-19

W
water 4, 20
white blood cells 12, 17, 18

About the Author

John Farndon is the author of a huge number of books for adults and children on science, history and nature, including international bestsellers, *Do Not Open* and *Do You Think You're Clever?*. He has been shortlisted for the Young People's Science Book Prize five times, including for the book *Project Body.*

About the Illustrator

Alan Rowe has been working as a freelance Illustrator since 1985. His work is heavily influenced by 1950s and 60s cartoons. Maybe all that time spent glued to the TV as a child wasn't all wasted!